Inspired by a character created by
S. M. Skolnick

Design by
Mullen & Katz

Copyright © 1997
Peter Pauper Press, Inc.
202 Mamaroneck Avenue
White Plains, NY 10601
All rights reserved
ISBN 0-88088-819-9
Printed in China
7 6 5 4 3 2

Dreidelcat

This is a story about two types of Jewish heroes. The Macca-cats, who fought the Greco-Syrians and took back the holy city of Jerusalem, were military and spiritual heroes. They stood up for their beliefs and resisted the outside aggressor.

Dreidelcat and his wife, Hannah, are modern Jewish heroes. In relating the story of Hanukah to their four small kittens, they keep the light of freedom burning brightly, for this generation, and the generations to come.

E. L.

There once was
a cat named Dreidel,
who lived in the village
of Kitten Hollow.

He was born on the
first night of Hanukah,
the 25th day of Kislev,
the day the Macca-cats
liberated Jerusalem from
the Greco-Syrians.

When Dreidelcat grew up and had a family of his own, he continued the tradition of retelling the story of Hanukah.

His wife, Hannah, and their four small kittens—

Nun,

Gimmel,

Heh, and

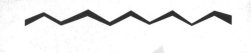

*S*hin—

One of the dogs
entered the Temple
and sacrificed a Cat
on the altar.

He forced them to worship all dogs and to eat what was alien to them as proof of their allegiance to him.

The desecration
of the Temple was
a cat-astrophe.

Enraged by this action,
an old Tabby named
Mattathias clawed the
hound to death.
A revolt had begun.

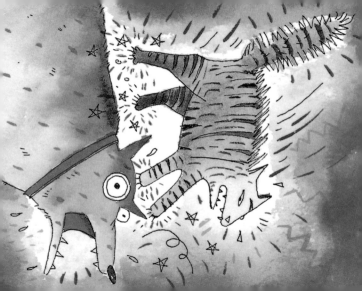

Pursued by the Greco-Syrian hound dogs, Mattathias and his five sons, known as the Macca-cats, fled to the hills surrounding Jerusalem. There the resistance movement took form.

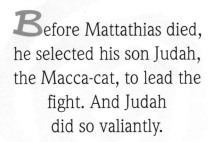

Before Mattathias died,
he selected his son Judah,
the Macca-cat, to lead the
fight. And Judah
did so valiantly.

Through strategy and foresight, the Cats overcame all of Antio-hound's forces, including an army riding armadillos.

In victory,
the Macca-cats liberated
Jerusalem from the
invaders, and on the 25th
day of Kislev they cleansed
the Temple.

According to legend, a miracle then occurred. To rededicate the Temple, holy oil was needed to light the Temple's great menorah, or candelabrum. The Jewish cats searched and searched, but found only one small cruse of sacramental oil, barely enough to last a day.

Knowing it would take eight days to prepare new holy oil, they nevertheless used the little bit of oil and lit the menorah. Miraculously, the oil burned for eight days! And that, along with the Macca-cats' victory, is what we celebrate today.

Dreidelcat's kittens
meowed with delight.
Having retold the story,
Dreidelcat lit
the menorah.

On the first night
Dreidelcat always
lit the Shamas with
his large paw.

Then his wife, Hannah, took the Shamas and lit the other candle, while everyone recited the prayers.

After lighting
the Shamas and as the other
candles are kindled,
the following blessings
are pronounced:

*Blessed is the Lord our God,
Ruler of the Universe, who hallows us with His Mitzvot, and
commands us to kindle the
Hanukah lights.*

*Blessed is the Lord our God,
Ruler of the Universe, who
performed wondrous deeds for
our ancestors in days of old,
at this season.*

(On the first night only, the following
blessing is also recited:)

*Blessed is the Lord our God,
Ruler of the Universe, for
granting us life, for sustaining
us, and for enabling us to
reach this season.*

Mewing, Dreidelcat and his family then sang "Rock of Ages" and, of course, "Dreidel, Dreidel," the family's favorite song.

The smiles on
the kittens' faces broadened
when Hannah brought
out a bowl of lat-cats
and applesauce.

They noshed
and washed and licked
their bowls clean.
What a pleasant way to
spend the first night
of Hanukah!

The four little kittens—
Nun, Gimmel, Heh, and
Shin—purred for joy.
Dreidelcat looked around
happily. He was very aware
of another miracle—the
miracle of a loving family.